40 DAYS IN THE WILDERNESS

–

40 DAYS IN THE WILDERNESS

In-depth personal reflections to nourish you as you
journey through the wilderness in the strong faith
needed to sustain you.

Rita Kroon

Seek the Lord to fill your empty cup with your daily
portion that you may be nourished and refreshed.

A Walk to the Well

Dedication

*My current works are written in
in loving memory of my husband, Burt,
and our daughter, Rene'
my other two daughters, LaDawn
and Shelly and their husbands,
my grandchildren,
my sister, Gayle, and
for all who have ever spent time in the
wilderness on their journey of life on earth.*

Rita Kroon

TABLE OF CONTENTS

INTRODUCTION

May this be your expectation every morning as you bring your empty cup before the Lord: that He would fill your cup with your **daily portion** from His Word that you may drink deeply and be nourished. *Lord, You have assigned me my portion and my cup. You have made my lot secure. Psalm 16:5*

Each day has a key verse for the topic at hand, but also includes passages to read before and after the selected verse in order to reveal its meaning within the context of Scripture. The **goal** of the passage of Scripture becomes clear, along with the **obstacles** that stand in the way of attaining the goal, **affirmations** that reinforce the truth of God's Word, a **personal application of the principles,** and the **results** where you will be able to determine if your results coincide with the goal of the passage. Two personal questions follow that you ask yourself in order to prayerfully examine your heart to determine if you are reaching your goal and discover what may be hindering you.

Fill your cup with your daily portion as a
day-by-day reminder of our
dependence on Jesus.
Fill your cup and be satisfied in the
Lord Jesus Christ.

When the people of Israel were delivered from four hundred years of captivity in Egypt, the LORD led them through the wilderness of Sinai to the Promised Land. But because of their rebellion against the LORD, they were made to wander for forty years. Yet, God did not abandon them. On the contrary, He provided for their every need. He provided water for them to drink and He nourished them with bread rained down from heaven. The Hebrews called this sweet, flaky, white substance 'manna'. Every morning, the people would gather only what each family needed for their **daily portion** to sustain them except on the day before the Sabbath when they would gather a double portion.

Are you in the wilderness? A drought in your spiritual walk, perhaps? A desert in your marriage with no oasis in sight? A dry spell at work or at school? Devoid of financial security? Lacking peace in a chaotic world? Suffering with poor health? Whatever your wilderness, take heart. This collection of forty daily devotionals will give insight to strengthen and to nourish you as you journey *through* the wilderness.

As a cup of cold water refreshes a parched throat, so it is with the Living Water that restores the weary soul of such a one who walks in the wilderness.

Day 1 ~ Obedience to the Lord

Read Exodus 3:7-4:31

Exodus. 3:10 *"Therefore, come now, and I will send you to Pharaoh so that you may bring My people, the sons of Israel, out of Egypt."*

Goal: To learn obedience to the Lord to do all He commands.

Obstacles: Fear of yielding to God, unbelief, feelings of uncertainty, apprehension that others would scoff at your commitment to the Lord, and feelings of

Affirmations: Moses recorded the words of God, "I AM WHO I AM," that demonstrates His power and His foreknowledge, and that He will provide all that is necessary to obey His commands.

Personal Application of Principles: Believers must clearly determine God's actual call to a specific task, and if so, we cannot worry whether other people will listen to or believe in our testimony of faith. If God has called us, our feelings of inadequacy and feelings of being unqualified are no excuse. We need not fear.

1

We can be assured that if God calls us to a task, He will supply us with all we need. To disobey God will certainly incur His wrath.

Result: We pray to strive to be obedient to the Lord in mind and heart to do what He has called us to do.

Ask yourself: What has God called me to do?

What obstacles am I facing and how can I overcome them?

Day 2 ~ Perfected and Strengthened

Read 1 Peter 5:5-10

1 Peter 5:6-7 *"Humble yourselves therefore under the mighty had of God so that at the proper time, He may exalt you; casting all your anxieties on Him because He cares for you. Be sober-minded, be alert, your adversary, the devil, prowls about like a roaring lion seeking someone to devou*r. (ESV)

Goal: To be perfected, strengthened, confirmed and established in my faith.

Obstacles: Pride, anxieties, suffering, and the devil.

Affirmations: Peter writes: God resists the proud but gives grace to the humble and will exalt them at the proper time. God cares for you. Resist the devil, be firm in your faith, knowing that the same kinds of suffering are being experienced by your brethren throughout the world. God is the God of all grace, and that God has called you. All believers are called to worship the Lord, but God also calls individuals to specific tasks specifically designed for each person.

Personal Application of Principles: If we, as believers, humble ourselves before God, He will give us grace and will exalt us at the proper time.

We know that God cares for us. We are to be sober-minded and alert to the devil, for we are enabled to resist him if we are firm in our faith. God is the God of all grace, and we can be confident that He has called us.

Result: God Himself will perfect, confirm, strengthen, and establish us in faith.

Ask yourself: How am I confirmed and established in the Lord?

How do I humble myself before the Lord?

Day 3 ~ A Heart Blameless to the Lord

Read 2 Chronicles 15:17-16:10

2 Chron. 16:9 *"For the eyes of the Lord run to and fro throughout the whole earth, to give strong support to those whose heart is blameless toward Him."* (ESV)

Goal: To have a heart blameless before the Lord.

Obstacles: Pride, looking to others for victory rather than seeking the Lord, and not standing firm under trial and testing because of fear.

Affirmations: Ezra records how God let Asa, king of Judah, find Him when he sought Him with all his heart, and God gave Judah peace from their enemies as long as Asa's heart and the hearts of the people were turned toward Him.

Personal Application of Principles: We must put aside all idols (anything that takes the rightful place of God) and seek the Lord with all our hearts especially in the midst of fear and anxiety. We are to humble ourselves before Him. We know our faith will be tested to see if we would turn to anyone apart from God for deliverance. We must put away pride and put on humility before the Lord.

Result: God is glorified, our hearts are blameless toward Him, and He will give us strong support.

<u>Ask yourself</u>: How can I be sure my heart is blameless before the Lord?

What idol do I have in my life that takes precedence over the Lord, and what will I do to rid the idol?

Day 4 ~ Receive the Word by Faith

Read Hebrews 3:12-4:3

Hebrews 4:2 *"For indeed, we have had good news preached to us, just as they also; but the word they heard did not profit them, because it was not united by faith in those who heard."*

Goal: To receive the Word by faith, and to enter His rest.

Obstacles: Hard hearts because of the deceitfulness of sin, disobedience, unbelief, little faith, and an evil unbelieving heart.

Affirmations: The author writes that there is hope as long as it is still called "Today", that we have become partakers of Christ, we have assurance (faith of things hoped for – the conviction of things not seen, Hebrews 11:1), we have good news preached to us, we who believe will enter His rest, we profit if we hear and believe, and heaven is sure,

Personal Application of Principles: When we hear the Word of Truth preached, we are to listen with an open ears and open heart. We cannot let sin enter in or deceive us, but we are to shun all evil. We believe that faith comes from hearing and hearing by the Word of God, so the more we listen to His Word, the more our faith will grow for without faith, it is impossible to please Him. We are intentional to keep our hearts tender to the Lord and not to provoke or test the Lord.

Result: We will receive the Word by faith, and we will enter His rest that was prepared before the foundation of the world.

Ask yourself: Why is it difficult for me to receive God's Word by faith?

What does God promise me if my faith is pleasing to Him?

Day 5 ~ Have No Fear

Read Isaiah 41:5-13

Isaiah 41:10 *"Do not fear for I am with you; do not anxiously look about you, for I am your God. I will strengthen you; surely I will help you; surely I will uphold you with My righteous right hand."*

Goal: To have no fear.

Obstacles: Enemies, discouragement, estranged from God, surrounding adverse circumstances, weakness, and sin.

Affirmations: Isaiah says that God is God and that He is with us, that as brothers encourage brothers so God gives encouragement, that God will strengthen us, God will help us, He will uphold us with His righteous right hand, He will defend us, He has called us, and God will take away our sin.

Personal Application of Principles: Whenever we are faced with threatening circumstances, we can know that God will deliver us. When we are troubled, we can be assured that God will encourage us and lift us up. When we are weak, God will give us strength, and when we need help, our help comes from the Lord. When we begin to waver, God will

9

uphold us, and when we are attacked by the enemy, God will defend us. When we are doubtful, God reassures us that He has called us, and when we feel the sting of sin, we can know that God has delivered us.

Result: We have no reason to fear.

Ask yourself: What is my greatest fear?

What is my greatest hindrance to peace, and how do I overcome such a hindrance?

Day 6 ~ Treasure the Words of God

Read Amos 8:1-12

Amos 8:11 *"Behold, days are coming," declares the Lord God, "When I will send a famine on the land, not a famine for bread or a thirst for water, but rather for hearing the words of the Lord."*

Goal: To treasure the Words of God at all times and in all seasons.

Obstacles: Ignoring the Word of God in prosperity, focusing on doing business, impatience on holidays to get back to business rather than to honor God on the day set aside to worship, losing sight of things that count for eternity, focusing on earthly gain, greed, and a famine of God's Words because of evil deeds done in the land.

Affirmations: Amos records the anger of the Lord that He has declared the end has come for Israel because of their evil deeds and because of their forsaking Him. God will cause the earth to quake and will bring about judgment. He causes a full eclipse of the sun as a sign of His judgment, and He will cause a famine of His words.

Personal Application of Principles: We must flee from sin and evil. We must be aware of God's coming judgment for evil and hold fast to God's words. We have the advantage during times of freedom and prosperity to read, meditate, and memorize the words of God and to focus on things that count for eternity. We must not allow ourselves to be pre-occupied with earthly matters.

Result: We will always treasure God's Word in all seasons - more so than we would be concerned with earthly matters.

<u>Ask yourself</u>: How can I make God's Word a priority and a treasure to me?

Why is it important for me to read and meditate on His Word especially during times of prosperity?

Day 7 ~ Fulfill the Law Through Love

Read Romans 13:8-14

Romans 13:8 *"Owe nothing to anyone except to love one another; for he who loves his neighbor has fulfilled the Law."*

Goal: To fulfill the Law through love.

Obstacles: Debt, hatred, adultery, murder, theft, covetousness, deeds of darkness, lust, carousing, drunkenness, promiscuity, sensuality, strife, and jealousy.

Affirmations: In his letter to the Romans, Paul writes that he who loves his neighbor has fulfilled the Law. You shall love your neighbor as yourself since love does no wrong, therefore, love is the fulfillment of the Law. Salvation is closer than when we first believed, so put on the armor of light and put on the Lord Jesus Christ.

Personal Application of Principles: We can overcome the deeds of darkness by putting on the armor of light which is the Word of Truth in the power of God. We can put on the Lord Jesus Christ

13

thereby loving those in need – our neighbor – as ourselves. If we walk in Jesus' love, we will have genuine love, and we will do no wrong to our neighbor.

Result: We will love our neighbor as ourselves and thereby fulfill the Law. We will only do good to our neighbor for his well-being.

<u>Ask yourself</u>: How am I fulfilling the Law through love?

How can I overcome the deeds of darkness?

Day 8 ~ Receive the Desires of Your Heart

Read Psalm 37:1-11

Psalm 37:4 *"Delight yourself in the Lord, and He will give you the desires of your heart."*

Goal: To receive the desires of one's heart.

Obstacles: Fretting over evildoers, envious of wrongdoers, lack of trust in the Lord, unfaithfulness, impatience, anger, wrath, fretting that leads to evil doing, and pride.

Affirmations: David says that the evildoers and the wrongdoers will wither like the grass and fade like the green herb. Delight yourself in the Lord and He will give you the desires of your heart, to commit your way to Him, and trust in Him, and He will do it. He will bring forth your righteousness as the light. Fretting over the evil one who prospers only leads to evil doing, but those who wait for the Lord (meek) will inherit the land. The wicked man will be no more, and the humble will delight themselves in abundant prosperity.

Personal Application of Principles: We dare not desire the prosperity or riches of those who made their gain by evil means. We shall trust in the Lord to provide all that we need. If we find our delight in the Lord, He will bless us. We shall commit our way to the Lord and we shall trust in Him with complete confidence of His faithfulness. He will bring forth righteousness, therefore, we will turn away from envy of the wicked ones' prosperity. If we will humble ourselves and wait for the Lord, we will find delight in the abundant prosperity in and through Jesus Christ.

Result: We will receive the desires of our hearts.

Ask yourself: What does it mean to pray with expectation?

How do I avoid being envious over one who prospers by evil gain?

Day 9 ~ Temptation or Testing

Read James 1:13-18

James: 1:13 *"Let no one say when he is tempted, 'I am being tempted by God'; for God cannot be tempted by evil and He Himself does not tempt anyone."*

Goal: To recognize the difference between temptation and testing.

Obstacles: Not being able to discern one's own lust from testing, following after lusts which leads to sin which in turn leads to death, being deceived, and believing a lie.

Affirmations: James declares that God does not change. God is perfect and gives perfect gifts, He gives truth, He rewards those who seek to obey His truths. God does not tempt anyone, but tests those whose faith needs strengthening.

Personal Application of Principles: We believe that God is perfect and does not change, that He gives perfect gifts, and rewards those who seek to obey Him. We are enabled to recognize temptation and our own bent to do evil. We are never tempted by God, but we are tested by Him through trials for our good. We can recognize that the strengthening of our faith is a result of the testing of our faith.

Result: We are able to recognize the difference between temptation and testing and respond accordingly.

Ask yourself: How do I recognize the difference between temptation and testing?

What is my greatest temptation and how do I respond to it?

Day 10 ~ Draw Near to God

Read James 4:1-10

James 4:7-8 *"Submit yourselves therefore to God. Resist the devil and he will flee from you. Draw near to God and He will draw near to you."* (ESV)

Goal: To draw near to God and for God to draw near.

Obstacles: Conflicts and quarrels among people, lust and murder, envy, wrong motives, selfishness, spiritual adultery, friendship with the world, pride, the devil, and turmoil within self.

Affirmations: James writes that the indwelling Holy Spirit longs jealously over us; that if you ask with selfish motives, you will not receive; that God gives a greater grace to the humble. If we resist the devil, he will flee, and if we draw near to God, He will draw near to us. He will exalt the humble.

Personal Application of Principles: Our inner conflict is caused by trying to have dual friendships – one with the world and one with God. To lust for evil pleasure or to be greedy for things is wrong. If we ask God with wrong motives, we will not receive. When we desire to be faithful, we can be confident that the Spirit longs jealously over us for our good. Our desire to be friends with God should far outweigh our desire to be friends with the world. We receive God's grace when we humble ourselves. We know that if we draw near to God and resist the devil, he will flee from us.

Result: We will draw near to God and He will draw near to us, and the devil will have no power over us.

Ask yourself: What is the benefit of drawing near to God?

How do I successfully resist the devil?

Day 11 ~ Fear Not Those Who Kill

Read Matthew 10:16-33

Matt. 10:28 *"And do not fear those who kill the body, but are unable to kill the soul; but rather fear Him who is able to destroy both soul and body in hell."*

Goal: To fear not those who kill the body.

Obstacles: Man who delivers us up to the courts, brothers deliver brothers to death, hatred, persecution, and fear.

Affirmations: Matthew records the words of Jesus that testimony will be given you at the time you need it, that whoever endures to the end will be saved, that Jesus will come again, that sins of the enemy will be found out. Man is not able to kill the soul. Your Father knows your tribulations and cares deeply, and that you are of more value to God than anything on earth.

Personal Application of Principles: We need not be anxious what we will say if we are called to give testimony of Jesus. We need not be anxious or fearful during perilous times because Jesus told us these things would happen, but rather, we are to endure persecutions to the end. We can hope in Jesus' return. We are encouraged by the Father's great love and His deep concern for us and that He will deliver us. We know God is sovereign. We can confidently confess Jesus before men.

Result: We need not fear those who can kill the body, but cannot kill the soul.

Ask yourself: What makes me fearful of harm or death from others? Why?

How can I overcome such fear?

Day 12 ~ Obey God Rather than Men

Read Acts 5:19-31

Acts 5:29 *"We must obey God rather than men."*

Goal: To obey God and to speak the message of life rather than to obey man's commands.

Obstacles: Imprisonment, persecution, believing false teachers, pressure from the adversary, and fear.

Affirmations: Luke records the example of how the angel of the Lord opened the prison gates and let the disciples out, how the angel told them to preach the message of life, and how the disciples obeyed. The Council was fearful of the blood of Jesus and commanded them not to teach in His name. Peter and the apostles were convinced that it was better to obey God rather than men.

Personal Application of the Principles: We need not be frightened at any opposition to the truth, but to speak and write the message of life with love and compassion for the lost. We know that God will protect us as we seek to be obedient to Him. We can learn from the disciples' example that God is faithful, that Jesus is the Christ, and that we too are messengers of God since we belong to Him.

Result: We will obey God and continue to write and speak the message of life in faith to the lost and hurting.

<u>Ask yourself</u>: How do I freely share the Gospel with others? If not, why not?

How do I overcome my main obstacle for not sharing the Gospel?

Day 13 ~ Obtain True Knowledge

Read Colossians 1:15-2:3

Col. 2:2 "...*that their hearts may be encouraged, having been knit together in love, and attaining to all the wealth that comes from the full assurance of understanding, resulting in a true knowledge of God's mystery, that is Jesus Christ Himself.*"

Goal: To obtain true knowledge.

Obstacles: Alienation from God, hostile in mind, doer of evil deeds, sin, lack of understanding spiritual matters, discouragement, and strife.

Affirmations: Paul tells us that Jesus is the image of the invisible God, and by Jesus all things were created, He was before all things and all things hold together in Him. Jesus is the head of the church and He has first place in everything. All the fullness of the Father dwells in Him. God reconciles all things to Himself through Jesus' shed blood on the cross. Jesus will present us blameless and beyond reproach to the Father. The mystery of God was hidden from ages past, namely Jesus Christ who is revealed to man. Jesus is the hope of glory, and we are complete in Christ. We have full assurance of understanding.

Personal Application of the Principles: We can know and trust that Jesus is the image of the invisible God and that He is eternal. It is revealed that all things were made by Him and for Him and that through His death, we are reconciled to God. We can be confident that Jesus will present us holy and blameless to His Father and that Jesus is our hope in glory.

Result: We are fully convinced that we have obtained the true knowledge of God's mystery: namely Jesus Christ.

<u>Ask yourself</u>: How have I obtained the true knowledge of God's mystery: Jesus Christ, the visible image of the invisible God?

What discourages me from seeking deeper knowledge of God?

Day 14 ~ Faith that Pleases God

Read Hebrews 11:1-12

Hebrews 11:6 *"And without faith it is impossible to please Him, for whoever comes to God must believe that He exists and that He rewards those who seek Him."*

Goal: To have faith that pleases God.

Obstacles: Unbelief, skepticism, jealousy, disrespect towards God, looking to worldly things for guidance and fulfillment, and difficult or seemingly impossible situations.

Affirmations: The author testifies that faith is the assurance of things hoped for – the assurance of things not seen, that Able and Enoch are mentioned as having faith, that faith is pleasing to God, that God rewards those who seek Him in faith, that Noah had faith and built an ark and saved his entire family from the flood, that Abraham had faith and it was counted to him as righteousness, and that Sarah had faith and thereby conceived a son long after her child-bearing years.

27

Personal Application of the Principles: We believe that God exists and that He created the heavens and the earth. He rewards those who seek Him so we can trust that we will receive rewards. By faith, we have eternal life through Jesus Christ. Because of faith, we are counted as righteous and it is through faith that we see our prayers answered.

Result: Our faith is pleasing to God, and brings salvation and rewards from God.

<u>Ask yourself:</u> How can I gain faith that pleases God?

Why is it impossible to please God without faith?

Day 15 ~ God's Good Pleasure

Read Philippians 2:5-16

Phil. 2:12-13 *"Therefore, my beloved, as you have always obeyed, so now, not only in my presence but much more in my absence, work out your own salvation with fear and trembling, for it is God who works in you, both to will and to work for His good pleasure.* (ESV)

Goal: To will and to work for God's good pleasure.

Obstacles: Bad attitude, disobedience, pride, grumbling and disputing, sin guilt, and living among a perverse generation.

Affirmations: Paul explains to the Philippians that Jesus existed in the form of God, but humbled Himself, not regarding equality with God to exploit for His own advantage. Jesus humbled Himself to the point of death on a cross. God highly exalted Jesus and bestowed on Him the name that is above every name so that at the name of Jesus, every knee will bend and every tongue confess that Jesus is Lord to the glory of the Father. It is God who works in us both to will (desire) and to work (action) so that we may prove ourselves blameless and innocent children of God. Even in a perverse generation, we are as lights in the world.

Personal Application of the Principles: We can know, though not understand fully, that Jesus is God in the flesh. We believe that at the mention of His name, every knee in heaven, on earth, and under the earth will bow before Him as Lord. We are to seek to be obedient to God – to desire to do God's good pleasure and not our own. In Jesus Christ, we will be blameless and innocent, and we are to be a light in a dark world.

Result: We will have a God-given desire to act/work for His good pleasure, to our salvation, and for His glory.

Ask yourself: As a steadfast believer, how can I truly desire to work for God's good pleasure?

What specific sins are blocking my desire to work for God's good pleasure and not for my own pleasures?

Day 16 ~ Become Children of God

Read 1 John 2:28-3:4

1 John 3:1 *"See how great a love the Father has bestowed upon us that we should be called children of God, and such we are."*

Goal: To become children of God – clothed in righteousness.

Obstacles: Sin, lawlessness, unrighteousness, guilt, and shame.

Affirmations: John writes that Jesus is righteous and that everyone who practices righteousness is born of Him. When He appears, we will have confidence and not shrink back in shame. The Father loves us with so great a love that He would call us children of God. When He appears, we shall be like Him for we shall see Him as He is. We fix our hope on Him and are purified by His blood just as He is pure.

Personal Application of the Principles: Because Jesus is righteous, we can practice righteousness since we are born of Him. We can have confidence of our righteousness through Him and not shrink back in shame at His appearing. We can know that the Father has such a great love for us in Jesus that we should be called children of God and if children, then heirs with Christ Jesus. When Jesus appears, we shall be like Him, and we shall see Jesus just as He is. We fix our hope on Jesus and purify ourselves just as He is pure.

Result: We are children of God clothed in righteousness.

<u>Ask yourself</u>: How do I know I am clothed in righteousness?

What could prevent me from being clothed in righteousness?

Day 17 ~ Resist Temptation to Sin

Read 1 Corinthians 10:1-13

1 Cor. 10:13 *"No temptation has overtaken you that is not common to man. God is faithful and will not let you be tempted beyond your ability, but with the temptation will provide the way of escape that you may be able to endure it."*

Goal: To resist the temptation to sin.

Obstacles: Craving of evil things, idolatry, immorality, testing the lord, grumbling, and arrogance.

Affirmations: In Paul's letter to the Corinthians, he asserts that all temptations are common to man; that there are no temptations that are new or that have not been experienced previously. God is faithful and will not allow us to be tempted beyond our ability, but will provide the way of escape which is Christ's death on the cross. Jesus' death overcame sin, and so we can resist the temptation to sin.

Personal Application of the Principles: Because Christ died for our sins, we are free from the snare of sin. We know that God is faithful to empower us to resist temptations and will provide the way of escape that we may be able to endure it.

Result: We can resist (overcome) the temptation to sin.

Ask yourself: How do I resist temptation on a consistent basis?

How does knowing that Christ died for my sins help me to resist temptation?

Day 18 ~ Crown of Life

Read James 1:2-12

James 1:4 *"And let endurance (steadfastness) have its perfect result that you may be perfect and complete, lacking in nothing."*

Goal: To receive the Crown of life.

Obstacles: Various trials, doubt, double-mindedness, unstable, pride, and pursuit of riches.

Affirmations: James says to consider it joy to encounter trials, to know that the testing of faith produces endurance, to let endurance have its perfect result, to understand that the testing of one's faith is designed to perfect one, so he is lacking nothing. We can know that God gives wisdom without reproach to those who ask in faith, and blessed is the one who perseveres under trial with approval from God.

Personal Application of the Principles: We are encouraged to encounter trials with joy. We know that the testing of our faith produces endurance which results in our completeness - lacking nothing. We are assured that if we ask God for wisdom, He

35

will give it to us without reproach. Our faith is undivided and we are strengthened to persevere under trial to meet God's approval.

Result: We will receive the crown of life which the Lord has promised to those who love Him.

Ask yourself: How can I be confident I will receive the crown of life and on what am I basing this?

How do I respond to trials in my life?

Day 19 ~ Stand Against Evil Schemes

Read Ephesians 6:10-18

Eph. 6:*11* *"Put on the whole armor of God that you may be able to stand against the schemes of the devil."*

Goal: To recognize and stand against the schemes of the devil.

Obstacles: Demonic hosts of Satan always assembled for mortal battle, the rulers, authorities, and world forces of evil in the heavenly places. To stand against the devil without faith and without being grounded in the Word is an unsurmountable obstacle.

Affirmations: Paul tells the Ephesians to put on the full armor of God, that God's armor equips them to combat spiritual evil forces, that they have as their equipment the truth, righteousness, the gospel, their faith, salvation, the Word of God, prayer, and the Holy Spirit. Paul's affirmations to be alert and to persevere are meant for us as well.

Personal Applications of the Principles: We are made aware of Satan's tactics and are provided with the very armor needed to combat him – not in our strength, but through the truth in God's Word, in righteousness, the gospel, our faith, our salvation, the Word of God, prayer, and the Holy Spirit. We are then, fully equipped.

Result: We can stand against the schemes of the devil in victory.

Ask yourself: By what means am I equipped to stand against the schemes of the devil?

What armor do I trust in?

Day 20 ~ Judge Not

Read Matthew 7:1-5

Matt. 7:1-2 *"Do not judge, lest you be judged. For the way you judge, you will be judged; and by your standard of measure, it will be measured to you."*

Goal: To affirm others and not to judge them.

Obstacles: Hypocrisy, censorship, impurity, critical spirit, controlling attitude, harshness, and pride.

Affirmations: Matthew gives the warnings of Jesus to his readers that in the way they judge others, they will be judged. The same standard used towards others will be the standard by which they are measured. We are to take the log out of our own eyes first, to purify ourselves, and then we will be able to help the one with the speck in his eye.

Personal Applications of the Principles: We are reminded of our own critical attitude and judgmental nature, and how hypocritical it is to the Lord. We know that when we criticize others, either in thought or by words said, it is displeasing to the Lord. We must be purified in our hearts and minds first, and then offer godly wisdom with love to someone who may have a speck in his/her eye. We must seek to be rid of all hypocrisy.

Result: We will affirm others rather than be judgmental towards them.

<u>Ask yourself:</u> In what ways do I judge others or be critical of them?

What makes it most difficult for me to affirm others?

Day 21 ~ Justification by Faith

Read Galatians 2:16-21

Gal. 2:16 "*...nevertheless knowing that a man is not justified by the works of the Law, but through faith in Christ Jesus, even we have believed in Christ Jesus, that we may be justified by faith in Christ, and not by the works of the Law; since by works of the Law shall no man be justified.*"

Goal: To fully grasp that justification is by faith.

Obstacles: Trying to be justified by the works of the Law, unbelief, unrighteousness, exhibiting legal obedience as a means of winning God's acceptance, old sinful nature that rules the heart, and the grace of God nullified by seeking to be obedient through the Law.

Affirmations: Paul writes to the Galatians saying that man is not justified by the Law, but that man is justified through faith in Jesus Christ. Christ lives within us, and the life we now live, we live by faith—not through works of the Law. We have been made separate from the reigning power of the old sinful life. We now have the freedom to experience the power of the resurrected life of Jesus Christ by

41

faith, and that Jesus loved us and delivered Himself up for us.

Personal Application of the Principles: Believers trying to win God's favor by being obedient to the Law is fruitless, and if we did so, we would nullify the grace of God. We are to live by faith in Jesus Christ, not by works. Because we have been set free from our old sinful nature, and now by faith have the freedom to experience to the fullest, the resurrection power of Jesus Christ.

Result: We are justified by faith in Christ Jesus.

Ask yourself: How can I be sure I am justified by faith in God's eyes?

What works are most likely to overshadow my faith?

Day 22 ~ Run the Race

Read Hebrews 11:17-12:2

Heb. 12:1 *"Therefore, since we are surrounded by so great a cloud of witnesses, let us also lay aside every weight, and sin which clings so closely, and let us run with endurance the race that is set before us."*

Goal: To run the race with endurance.

Obstacles: Unbelief, desire for riches, rebellion, disobedience, unrighteousness, persecution, and sin.

Affirmations: The author of Hebrews affirms that because we have a great company of witnesses who lived by faith, we also lay aside every encumbrance and sin. We have many examples of people of faith and are encouraged by their endurance against deeds of darkness and unbelief, and so, we lay aside everything that entices us from God and look to the reward in Jesus. We fix our eyes on Jesus and the joy of running the race just as Jesus who for the joy set before Him endured the cross despising its shame and sat down at the right hand of God.

43

Personal Application of the Principles: We are encouraged by all those before us who lived by faith even in the harshest of circumstances. We are made aware of every encumbrance and sin that would trip us up. If we focus on Jesus, that is, to fix our eyes on Him, the author and perfecter of our faith, we will find joy in Him.

Result: We can run with endurance the race set before us.

Ask yourself: How can I obtain endurance to finish the race, and what is meant by the 'race'?

How am I depending on faith for the needed endurance?

Day 23 ~ Keep Oneself in the Love of God

Read Jude 12-23

Jude 20-21 *"But you, beloved, build yourselves up in your most holy faith; praying in the Holy Spirit; keeping yourselves in the love of God, waiting anxiously for the mercy of our Lord Jesus Christ to eternal life."*

Goal: To keep oneself in the love of God.

Obstacles: Pride, greed, rebellion, dead faith, rejecting God and His offer for forgiveness through Jesus Christ, deceit, covetousness, grumbling, finding fault, arrogance, flattering for self-gain, mocking, lusts, ungodliness, and worldly mindedness.

Affirmations: Jude defends the faith when he writes to 'build yourselves up on your most holy faith' which means to pray in the Spirit, to wait anxiously for the mercy of our Lord Jesus Christ to eternal life, and to have mercy on those who are living outside of God's love.

Personal Applications of the Principles: We can put aside all pride, greed, and rebellion and seek God's forgiveness of sins through His provision – namely Jesus Christ. Forsaking all ungodliness, we build ourselves up in our faith as we strive to pray in the Holy Spirit waiting eagerly for the mercy of our Lord Jesus Christ to eternal life. We are to show mercy on those who doubt and even on the vilest of people.

Result: We will keep ourselves in the love of God.

Ask Yourself: How am I keeping myself in the love of God?

What are my biggest obstacles living in the love of God?

Day 24 ~ Love from a Pure Heart

Read 1 Timothy 1:3-11

1 Tim. 1:5 *"But the goal of our instruction is love from a pure heart, a good conscience, and a sincere faith."*

Goal: To show love from a pure heart.

Obstacles: False doctrines, speculation and fruitless discussion, lawlessness, rebellion, ungodliness, murder, immorality, homosexuality, kidnapping, lying, and perjury.

Affirmations: Paul's letter to Timothy states that teaching truth and furthering the administration of God is by faith. The Law is made to expose the sins of the ungodly, and to show that the gospel of God is glorious.

Personal Application of the Principles: We can learn to listen to sound teaching and truth. We know that the furthering of the administration of God is by faith, and we recognize that the Law is good if we use it lawfully.

47

Result: We can love from a pure heart, a good conscience, and a sincere faith.

Ask yourself: In what ways can I show love from a pure heart?

How do I obtain a good conscience and a sincere faith?

Day 25 ~ Forgiveness

Read Ephesians 4:25-32

Eph. 4:32 *"And be kind to one another, tender-hearted, forgiving each other just as God in Christ also has forgiven you."*

Goal: To receive and to give forgiveness.

Obstacles: Lying, pent-up anger, theft, selfishness, bitterness, wrath, clamor, slander, and malice.

Affirmations: Paul says to speak truth with our neighbors, to let go of anger quickly, to work and share with those in need, to speak words good for edifying others, to put away all bitterness, wrath, and slander, to be kind to one another, to seek to be forgiven or to forgive those who seek forgiveness from us. We are to remember that God in Christ has forgiven us.

Personal Application of the Principles: If we speak truth to others, we eliminate a cause for anger from them. Also, if we harbor angry feelings, it only leads to bitterness and resentment, so we are to let go of our anger. If we slander someone, we are the cause of strife and in the same way, if others

49

slander us, we need to consider a proper response. We are to be kind to one another – tenderhearted and forgiving. We are to remember that God in Christ forgave us.

Result: We will know forgiveness.

<u>Ask yourself</u>: In what ways do I fail to be a forgiving person?

Could unresolved anger be causing me to become bitter?

Day 26 ~ To Be Justified

Read Romans 3:19-28

Rom. 3:23-24 *"...for all have sinned and fall short of the glory of God, and are justified by His grace as a gift, through the redemption that is in Christ Jesus."* (ESV)

Goal: To be justified.

Obstacles: Seeking justification through the works of the Law, sin, unbelief, unrighteousness, and lack of conformity to the glory of God.

Affirmations: Paul explains that through the Law comes the knowledge of sin and the need for a Savior. The righteousness of God was manifested in Jesus Christ, and this righteousness is obtained through faith in Christ, that is, being justified (declared righteous) is a gift of God's grace through the redemption which is in Jesus. The sinner who believes in Christ receives God's gift of righteousness and is justified by faith apart from the works of the Law.

Personal Application of the Principles: We have become aware of our sin through the Law and see our hopeless, sinful state, and our desperate need for a Savior. The righteousness that we need was manifested in Christ Jesus, and we obtain it as a gift by God's grace through faith in Christ Jesus. Everyone has sinned and has fallen far short of God's glory, but everyone who believes in Jesus Christ receives the gift of righteousness apart from the works of the Law.

Result: We are justified by faith as a gift.

Ask yourself: How am I justified in God's eyes?

What am I depending on for my justification - good works of the Law or pursuit of faith? Explain.

Day 27 ~ Forgiveness of Sins

Read Hebrews 9:15-28

Hebrews 9:22 *"And according to the Law, one may almost say, all things are cleansed with blood, and without the shedding of blood there is no forgiveness."*

Goal: To have forgiveness of sins.

Obstacles: If there is no mediator of the new covenant, there is no forgiveness of sins. If Jesus had not died, there would be no covenant, and if Jesus had not shed His blood, there would be no forgivness.

Affirmations: The author writes that because Jesus is the Mediator of a new covenant, and since He shed His blood and died for the redemption of man, He ratified the new covenant. Those who have been called may receive the promise of the eternal inheritance. Without the shedding of blood, there is no forgiveness of sins. Christ entered heaven itself and is in the presence of God as Mediator for us. It was neessary for Jesus to suffer and die once for all, and He shall appear a second time for salvation without reference to sin.

Personal Application of the Principles: We can know and trust in the fact that Jesus is the Mediator between God and man and by shedding His blood and dying, He ratified the covenant for the forgiveness of sins once for all.

Result: We can be fully assured of our total forgiveness of sins and can eagerly wait, without shame or guilt, His second coming in which He will take the redeemed sinners to Himself.

Ask Yourself: How can I be sure I am counted among the redeemed?

Does Christ Jesus' return comfort me or challenge me? Why?

Day 28 ~ Freedom

Read Galatians 5:13-25

Gal. 5:18 *"But if you are led by the Spirit, you are not under the Law."*

Goal: To have freedom.

Obstacles: Turning freedom into an opportunity for the flesh, biting and devouring one another, not walking by the Spirit, war between the Spirit and the flesh, deeds of the flesh which include all sins, boastful, challenging one another, and envy.

Affirmations: Paul's letter to the Galatians is a call to freedom, to love their neighbor as themselves, to walk by the Spirit that they would not carry out the deeds of the flesh, and to know that if led by the Spirit, they are not under the Law. Evidence (fruit) of the Spirit is love, joy, peace, patience, kindness, goodness, faithfulness, gentleness, and self-control, and there is no law against such things. Those who belong to Christ have crucified the flesh. To live by the Spirit and to walk by the Spirit applies to us as well.

Personal Application of the Principles: We are called to freedom. We were never intended to be in bondage. If we walk by the Spirit, we will live by the Spirit and will produce the fruit of the Spirit against which there is no law. Therefore, since we belong to Christ, we have put to death the sinful desires of the flesh.

Result: We have freedom from the Law because Christ has set us free.

Ask yourself: How can I be confident I have freedom from condemnation of the law and am no longer in bondage?

Hat does it mean to me to walk in the Spirit?

Day 29 ~ Justification by Faith

Read Galatians 3:17-26

Gal. 3:24 *"Therefore, the Law has become our tutor (attendant/custodian) to lead us to Christ that we may be justified by faith."*

Goal: To be confident that my salvations is by faith in Jesus Christ and Him only

Obstacles: Basing justification on the Law as a means to eternal life, unrighteousness, and unbelief.

Affirmations: Paul writes that the Law does not invalidate the covenant with Abraham made by God, but that the Law was added because of transgressions. The Law has become our tutor and custodian to lead us to Christ. The Law cannot impart life, but rather leads us to the One who gives life – Jesus Christ. The promise by faith in Jesus is given to those who believe, and since faith has come, we no longer need to be under a tutor. Therefore, we who believe are all sons of God through faith in Jesus Christ.

Personal Application of the Principles: We have been set free from the Law in order to believe in Christ Jesus through faith. The Law is to show us our sins and point us to the One who can forgive us since He fulfilled the Law on our behalf. We believe in Jesus and so the promise to be sons of God is given to us.

Result: We are justified by faith in Christ Jesus.

Ask yourself: What does it mean to me to base my justification on faith in Jesus Christ?

How am I set free from bondage under the Law?

Day 30 ~ Saving Faith

Read Romans 10:8-17

Romans 10:17 *"So faith comes from hearing and hearing by the word of Christ."*

Goal: To have saving faith

Obstacles: Unbelief, unrighteousness, not listening, and rejecting what is heard.

Affirmations: Paul says plainly that the word is near - ready for man to take on his lips and into his heart, and if we confess Jesus as Lord (deity) and believe, we will be saved. With the heart, man believes and is counted as righteousness, and with the mouth he confesses resulting in salvation. Whoever believes in Him will not be disappointed, and whoever calls upon the name of the Lord will be saved. Faith comes from hearing the spoken word of God and believing its truth.

Personal Application of the Principles: The word of God is near and if we listen with opened ears and believe, our faith is made sure. When we speak the word of Christ to others, we are confessing Jesus

Christ as Lord for we speak what we believe in our hearts, and whoever hears our testimony and believes, will be saved.

Result: We have saving faith and those who hear and believe have saving faith.

Ask yourself: What is meant by saving faith?

In what ways do I proclaim Jesus Christ as my Lord to others?

Day 31 ~ Fear the Lord

Read Deuteronomy 6:16-25

Deut. 6:24 *"So the Lord commanded us to observe all these statutes, to fear the Lord our God for our good always and for our survival, as it is today."*

Goal: To fear the Lord.

Obstacles: Grumbling and complaining for His provision, disobedience, arrogance, pride, and selfishness.

Affirmations: Moses spoke to the people saying, "You shall diligently keep the commandments of the Lord, you shall do what is right and good, and give glory to God for His deliverance from bondage. Obedience and fear to the Lord is for your good. It will be counted as righteousness for us if we are careful to observe this entire commandment."

Personal Application of the Principles: We are made aware of the gravity of grumbling and complaining against the Lord for His provision for us, and how that causes the Lord's anger to rise up.

61

Obedience is pleasing to the Lord. When we humble ourselves and glorify God for His deliverance from whatever bondage we may be in, we will be blessed beyond measure. It is to our benefit to fear the Lord – to show deepest respect, not fright or dread. When we are diligent and intentional about obedience, it is counted as righteousness to us.

Result: We will fear the Lord our God and we will be pleasing to Him.

Ask yourself: What does it mean to me to fear the Lord?

What am I most likely to complain about?

Day 32 ~ Heart of Compassion

Read Colossians 3:5-17

Col. 3:12 *"And so, as those who have been chosen of God, holy and beloved, put on a heart of compassion, kindness, humility, gentleness, and patience."*

Goal: To have a heart of compassion.

Obstacles: Immorality, impurity, evil desires, greed (which all amount to idolatry), anger, wrath, malice, slander, abusive speech, lying, and unforgiveness.

Affirmations: In his letter to the Colossians, Paul said to put on the new self who is being renewed to a true knowledge according to the image of the One who created him - those chosen by God: holy and beloved. Put on a heart of compassion, kindness, humility, gentleness and patience. Bear with one another, forgiving one another as the Lord forgave you. Put on love and let the peace of Christ rule in your hearts. Be thankful, and let the word of Christ dwell in you richly.

Personal Application of the Principles: We see that passion without holiness is evil and amounts to idolatry which brings God's wrath. Therefore, as chosen people of God, we put on the new self – renewed to a true knowledge according to the image of the One who created us. We put on compassion, kindness, humility, gentleness, patience, forgiveness, love, and we let the love of Christ rule in our hearts. We do all things in the name of the Lord Jesus Christ with thanksgiving.

Result: We have a heart of compassion.

Ask yourself: How does my heart of compassion display itself to others?

How do I put on the new self?

Day 33 ~ Obedience

Read Joshua 5:13-6:16

Joshua 6:3 *"And you shall march around the city, all the men of war circling the city once. You shall do this for six days."*

Goal: To capture the fortified city of Jericho through obedience.

Obstacles: The city was tightly shut in behind huge walls and fear.

Affirmations: Joshua writes of the time he saw a man standing with his sword drawn. When Joshua asked if he was friend or foe, the man said he was the captain of the host of the Lord. and that Joshua was to remove his shoes because he was standing on holy ground. The Lord told Joshua that He had given Jericho into his hand. Joshua was given specific instructions regarding the march around the city, and on the seventh lap around the city, he was to blow the trumpet and the walls would fall.

Personal Application of the Principles: When we are faced with a seemingly impossible task, we need not fear. We need only to be obedient to follow precisely the Lord's instruction. We can put aside fear and take up obedience with complete trust that the Lord will accomplish His purpose.

Result: We desire to strive for total surrender and complete obedience to the Lord.

Ask yourself: What huge task am I facing and how will I move forward?

Where am I failing to be obedient in all that the Lord commands me?

Day 34 ~ Fear Not - Worry Not

Read Luke 12:21-34

Luke 12:32 *"Fear not, little flock, for it is your Father's good pleasure to give you the kingdom."* (ESV)

Goal: To fear not and worry not.

Obstacles: Storing up earthly treasures and not being rich toward God, anxious for this life as to what to eat or what to drink or what to wear, lack of faith, worry, trusting in riches, and greed.

Affirmations: Luke wrote that life is more than food and the body is more than clothing. God feeds the birds, and He will provide for you because you are of more value than the birds. You cannot add a single hour to your span of life by being anxious, and since Gods clothes the grass of the fields with beautiful lilies, He will clothe people. Do not worry. Seek God's kingdom first, and all these things will be added unto you. That it is your Father's good pleasure to give you the kingdom.

Personal Application of the Principles: It is foolish for us to try to store up earthly treasures when we can be rich towards God. It is needless for us to have anxiety or to worry over food, or drink, or clothing since we are assured that our heavenly Father will provide our every need if we seek Him above all else, and those who are blessed with much have a God-appointed obligation to help the poor and needy. We can delight to know that God takes great pleasure in giving us the kingdom. We can rest in His abundant provision for us and for others through us.

Result: We need not fear, or worry, or be anxious.

Ask yourself: What do I fear or worry about the most?

Why is it foolish to trust in earthly riches?

Day 35 ~ Live by Faith

Read Romans 1:16-23

Rom. 1:16-17 *"For I am not ashamed of the Gospel for it is the power of God for salvation to everyone who believes, to the Jew first and also to the Greek. For in it the righteousness of God is revealed from faith for faith, as it is written, 'The righteous shall live by faith."* (ESV)

Goal: To live by faith.

Obstacles: Unbelief, unrighteousness, suppressed truth, no honor to God, futile in the mind, dark hearts, and idolatry.

Affirmations: Paul presented the gospel of Christ as the power of God for salvation to everyone who believes. The gospel reveals the righteousness of God for faith, and it is the righteous one who lives by faith. God's wrath is against all ungodliness and unrighteousness. God clearly revealed His invisible attributes, His eternal power, and His divine nature in the creation of the earth, and so the rejection of this truth makes one without excuse before God. God is incorruptible.

Personal Application of the Principles: Believers are not ashamed of the Gospel of Christ because we know it is the power of God unto salvation and reveals the righteousness of God. We can clearly recognize God's invisible attributes, His eternal power, and His divine nature in the creation of all things, and we can honor God in our hearts.

Result: We live by faith.

Ask yourself: Think of a situation when you had no recourse and no options but only to live by faith. Explain.

How does the creation of the universe, with its many unanswered mysteries, challenge or strengthen my faith?

Day 36 ~ Sufficient Grace

Read 2 Corinthians 12:6-10

2 Cor. 12:9 *"And He said to me, 'My grace is sufficient for you, for my power is made perfect in weakness.'"* (ESV)

Goal: To learn that God's sufficient grace can give contentment in my weakness.

Obstacles: Boastful of one's own strength, exalting self, wanting physical comforts above the power of Christ, and not wanting or willing to accept things that must be.

Affirmations: Paul said that because of the surpassing greatness of the revelations received and to prevent him from becoming boastful about such things, a thorn in the flesh was given to him that he should be reminded of his own human frailty and weaknesses. Paul had to recognize that it is the power of God that accomplishes all things. Paul said that to know and accept this truth is the beginning of understanding God's grace and therefore, one can be content with his weaknesses, insults, hardships, persecutions, and calamities because the power of Christ is made evident in his weakness.

Personal Application of the Principles: There is a danger of becoming prideful or boastful because of one's surpassing knowledge received. To prevent this, God may give a thorn in our flesh as a reminder of our weakness and of His power. When we recognize this and accept what must be – the thorn in the flesh – is when we can begin to understand what God means when He says, "My grace is sufficient for you." We are content with our weaknesses. We rejoice that the power of Christ is made evident in our weakness.

Result: We recognize that God's grace is sufficient, and we can be content in our weakness.

Ask yourself: Why is God's grace sufficient for me? Why or why not?

What is my thorn in the flesh, and how do I respond to it?

Day 37 ~ Contentment in Godliness

Read 1 Timothy 6:6-15

1 Tim. 6:6 *"But godliness actually is a means of great gain, when accompanied by contentment."* (ESV)

Goal: To find contentment in godliness.

Obstacles: Desire to get rich, temptations, foolish desires, love of money, unbelief, disobedience, and seeking riches over godliness.

Affirmations: Paul affirmed to Timothy that godliness is a means of great gain when accompanied by contentment. Therefore, be content if you have food and clothing. Flee from unrighteousness and fight the good fight. You were called to eternal life, and God gives life to all things. Jesus Christ will appear at the proper time, and Jesus is King of kings and Lord of lords.

Personal Application of the Principles: The righteous take seriously the warning that those who desire to get rich over being godly are in danger of falling away from the faith. We are to flee from evil and pursue righteousness, godliness, faith, love, perseverance, and gentleness. We are to fight the good fight, take hold of the eternal life to which we are called, and without stain or reproach, we are to keep the commandment.

Result: We will find contentment in godliness.

<u>Ask yourself</u>: What does it take for me to be content in godliness?

'

In what area(s) of my life do I lack godly contentment?

Day 38 ~ Exultant Living

Read Romans 8:26-39

Rom. 8:31 *"What then shall we say to these things? If God if for us, who is against us?"*

Goal: To learn what exultant living entails.

Obstacles: Not knowing how we should pray snf obstacles that overshadow who we are in Christ Jesus.

Affirmations: Paul writes that the Spirit helps us in our weaknesses, Jesus intercedes for us according to God's will, God causes all things to work together for good, we are called according to His purposes, those He foreknew, He predestined to be conformed to the image of His Son, and these He called, He justified, and He glorified. God is for us, and He will freely give us all things. God justifies us, and nothing can separate us from the love of Christ, and we are abundantly able to conquer through Him who loves us.

Personal Application of the Principles: Since the Spirit helps us in our weakness, and Jesus intercedes for us, we can know that God works all things together for good. God glorified those He justified, those He called, and the ones He foreknew, are the same. He predestined all believers to be conformed to the image of His Son. We can be assured that nothing can separate us from the love of Christ. We are told that difficulties are not necessarily obstacles for us as God's children, but His appointed way. Therefore, we can conquer through Him who loves us.

Result: We have exultant living.

Ask yourself: How can I experience exultant living?

If God is for me, who or what is distracting me from exultant living?

Day 39 ~ Faith Like a Mustard Seed

Read Luke 17:1-6

Luke 17:6 *"And the Lord said, 'If you had faith like a mustard seed, you would say to this mulberry tree, "Be uprooted and be planted in the sea," and it would obey you.'"*

Goal: To have faith like a mustard seed

Obstacles: Stumbling blocks, sin, unforgiveness, and lack of faith.

Affirmations: Luke draws attention to the fact that stumbling blocks are inevitable and to be alert to them. If your brother sins seven times a day against you, and repents, forgive him. Ask for increase of faith, and if you have faith even as small as a mustard seed, you could say to a mulberry tree to be uprooted and planted in the sea, and it would obey.

Personal Application of the Principles: As believers, we know there will always be stumbling blocks (temptations to sin), but we are to be on guard against them and to be careful not be a stumbling block to another. We are to forgive our brother as many times as he may sin against us, repents, and asks to be forgiven. As believers, we have the right to ask Christ Jesus to increase our faith, but even if our faith is only the size of a mustard seed, it would be enough to say to a mulberry tree to be uprooted and planted in the sea – and it would be so - something impossible for man to do, but possible with God.

Result: We will have true faith in the power of God even though our faith is like the size of a mustard seed.

Ask yourself: What does a measure of faith like a mustard seed look like?

To what could my faith be compared?

Day 40 ~ Be Strong & Courageous

Read Joshua 1:1-9

Joshua 1:9 *"Have I not commanded you? Be strong and courageous. Do not be frightened, and do not be dismayed, for the Lord your God is with you wherever you go."* (ESV)

Goal: To be strong and courageous

Obstacles: Physical deterrents, feelings of inadequacy, and fear.

Affirmations: Joshua recorded how Moses had previously told the people that Joshua would be the one to lead the people into the Promised Land, that God Himself would go with him would not forsake him. God said that no man would prevail against him, Joshua could _see_ the Promised Land beyond the Jordan, and that he had the promises of God.

Personal Application of the Principles: As we seek to obey God, we may encounter physical obstacles, but as we wait upon the Lord for affirmations either through His Holy Spirit, His Word, or other godly people, we have the promises of God that He will go with us and that he will not forsake us. We can be strong and courageous, not fearful or dismayed. When we meditate on His Word, we will be careful to do all that it says.

Results: We will be strong and courageous and will have success in whatever it is that God has called us to do.

Ask yourself: How have I seen success as a result of my obedience to God?

What are my greatest obstacles?

"The Lord is my portion," says my soul.

Therefore, I have hope in Him."

Lamentations 3:24

Dear Lord, You have led me through
the wilderness, You have refreshed me
and strengthened me, and
You are faithful to never forsake me,
and for that I give You
much thanksgiving.
You alone are the Supplier
of all my needs and my soul
knows it very well.

Meet the Author

Rita Kroon was born in Minneapolis, but raised in St. Paul, MN. She graduated from Sibley High School and received her AA degree in speech/ communications from Lakewood Comm. College.

She is an author, blogger, and Bible study leader. She has written wildlife magazine articles, children's short stories, poetry, devotionals, Bible studies, a humorous newspaper column "Rita Raps it Up," and Christian novels.

Rita writes in memory of her husband, Burt, and their daughter, Rene'. She has two other daughters, LaDawn and Shelly, and has 17 grandchildren. Rita lives in Lexington, MN,

Other Books by Rita Kroon

40 Days of Assurance is a daily devotional intended to give assurance in your walk with God, with parenting skills, with relationships, or with a lack of confidence with who you are as a person. Sometimes we just need loving arms around us; to be assured that everything will work out. Bring your empty cup to the Lord that He may fill it with your daily portion of His grace and mercy and discover the peace of God that surpasses all understanding that will keep your heart and mind in Christ Jesus. **ISBN: 9780989198530**

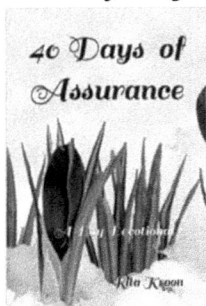

40 Days of Encouragement is a daily devotional for those times you may feel like giving up, or you are bombarded with negative thoughts, or you have lost all hope, or you are despairing over a broken relationship, or you see the future through the bleakness of the past. Be encouraged. God is a reservoir of strength. God has plans to give you a future and a hope. Come. Drink deeply of God's word and be encouraged.
ISBN: 9780989198547

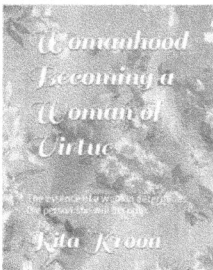

Womanhood: Becoming a Woman of Virtue is an interactive Bible study of eight inspirational women of the Old Testament and is suitable for individual or group setting. There are two sections: a twenty-week, in-depth study for the woman who likes to linger in the Word and an eight-week, con-densed study for the woman on the go. Explore the lives of Eve, Sarah, Rebekah, Rachel, Miriam, Deborah, Tamar, and Esther who are ordinary women who find themselves in unprecedented circumstances. Be inspired by their faith, encouraged through their hardships, and challenged by their choices and decisions as you seek to become a woman of virtue.

ISBN: 9780989198554

Kiss Your Mommy Goodbye is a Christian novel. In his desperate quest to provide love and stability as a part-time father to young Maddy, Mike does the unthinkable. His actions got far more disastrous results than he could have ever imagined, and the very one he tried to protect would suffer the repercussions of his decision. In this riveting tale, a divorced man struggles to reconcile and rebuild broken relationships and find peace with others and with God.   **ISBN: 9780989198561**

Cancer–a Journey through the Valley is a personal memoir. Rita Kroon shares her journey through the valley where she realized that her faith in God during the calm seasons of life necessitated a mighty strengthening if it was to sustain her on the battlefield. Discover how God worked such a faith while she was in the throes of cancer. Be amazed at the sovereignty of God to heal some and stand in awe to see His grace given to those for whom He has a different purpose. This is a story of hope and trust.

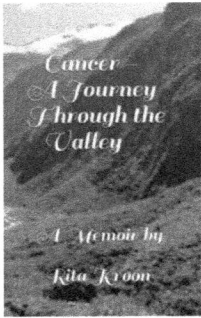

ISBN: 9780989198516

Letters from the Past is historical fiction. Eight women of the Bible write personal letters to today's woman. Each woman reveals the emotional impact that infertility, rape, incest, deception, betrayal, and family dysfunction had on her. In each of their stories, trial turns to triumph when the thread of God's faithfulness is traced through these women of ancient times to the women of the twenty first century. Today's woman will be challenged and encouraged, she will find hope for the oppressed, and will celebrate the accomplishments of Eve, Sarah, Rebekah, Rachel, Miriam, Deborah, Tamar, and Esther. **ISBN: 9780989198578**

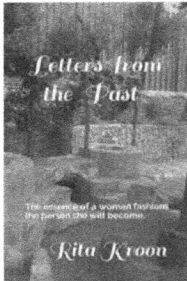

Praying the Scriptures is a collection of prayers
and promises taken from God's
Word, since no word of God
shall be void of power. When
words cannot be found to say
what is on your heart, this
collection of prayers is meant to
guide you during those times of
solitude. If praying is unfamiliar
to you, or perhaps has long ago
been abandoned, this book
provides one way to begin afresh. There is no
prayer like that which forms itself in the words and
thoughts of Scripture, for there are no other words
on earth spoken by man that have neither more
power nor more truth than God's Word.

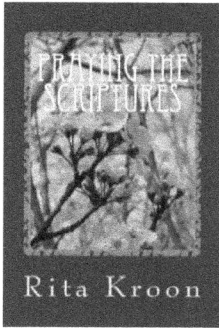

ISBN: 9780989198585

Discover God through His Attributes is an inspirational book meant to guide you in the search for a deeper and more meaningful relationship with God. Discover who He is. Be filled with awe. Give praise to the Creator of the heavens and the earth. Reverence Him for who He is, for there is no other god or anything in the entire universe like Him. Worship the King of kings in the splendor of His holiness. Rejoice that the Lord is one God as you discover the Father, Son, and Holy Spirit through His attributes.

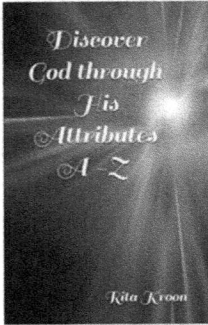

ISBN: 9780989198523

Nuggets From My Pocket is a collection of tidbits of wisdom, blessings, sayings, quotes, promises and more that have been gathered along the trail. These gems of truth will inspire and encourage you. They will give you cause to pause, a time to wonder and ponder, and a reason to reflect.

Here's a nugget to ponder: "God gives evidence of His existence, but not proof since He always leaves room for faith.

ISBN: 9780989198592

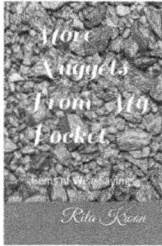

More Nuggets From My Pocket is a collection of sayings, wit, insights, quotes, wisdom, promises, prayer, and more that were gathered where the trail led to an open meadow.

These gems will inspire you and encourage you no matter what path of life you travel. Stop to ponder the insights given, or to discover a fresh perspective, or to glean new meaning to old sayings.

ISBN: 9798682187225

Extra Nuggets From My Pocket is a collection of sayings meant to stir your imagination, fill your heart, and satisfy your desire for fresh "Ah, moments."

When the path of life leads you beside still waters, search the beach for Extra Nuggets like one does when looking for agates on the North Shore. Some of these gems of truth, wit, quotes, prayers, blessings, and more are mine and some are those I gathered along the way and tucked into my pocket.

ISBN: 9798587330566

Almost-Forgotten Nuggets is a collection of truthful, inspiring, and wise sayings, and follows the footprints of its three siblings, *Nuggets From My Pocket, More Nuggets From My Pocket*, and *Extra Nuggets From My Pocket.* The path is familiar, but the landscape gives an added dimension of newness that makes a pleasant journey a most memorable one.

Here's a preview: "It is sometimes difficult, but always good, to trust God with who you treasure most in this world." Here's another: "Unconfessed sin is like a math problem: it divides the heart, adds woes, subtracts peace, and multiplies consequences." Come. Savor the Almost-Forgotten Nuggets.

ISBN:9798511772042

Pebbles of Truth is a collection of short, timeless sayings of truth that are filled with wisdom, give

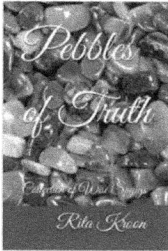

great insight, plus unforgettable blessings, quotes, encouragement, thoughts to remember, and explore God's greatness. These pebbles of truth connect the heart with one's imagination much like pebbles on a beach connect the water and the land.

Here's a sneak peek: "Learn to write your hurts in the sand and to carve your blessings in stone." Here's another: "Man contributed nothing to his salvation except the sin that made it necessary." Pebbles of Truth is sure to give you a delightful reading and sharing experience.

ISBN: 9798842917037

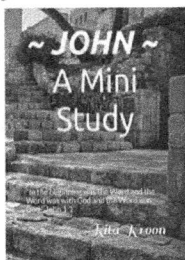

John – A Mini Study is a thirteen-week, interactive Bible study of the Gospel of John, and is suitable for individual or group setting. It uses an Observation-Interpretation-Application method of study in an easy-to-read format. One way to think of it is like this: The observation of facts is like reading a menu; the interpretation is looking at the number of calories or the price on the menu. Each application question is the main course – the most satisfying part of the meal that energizes us for action. Each lesson has a principle that helps to keep the participants focused on what the author is trying to convey. There are personal application questions and discussion questions to get the most out of studying God's Word.

We learn what we can, apply what we know, and leave the rest to God.

"This is the disciple who testifies of these things and wrote these things, and we know this testimony is true." John 21:24   "BEHOLD! The Lamb of God!"

ISBN: 9798545633234

A Walk to the Well –
A Place for Women to find
Encouragement, Hope, and Inspiration

www.awalktothewell.com

www.ingramcontent.com/pod-product-compliance
Lightning Source LLC
Chambersburg PA
CBHW071453070426
42452CB00039B/1345